RENEWABLE ENERGY

BY HARRIET BRUNDLE

PLANET EARTH HELPERS

BookLife
PUBLISHING

©2020
BookLife Publishing Ltd.
King's Lynn
Norfolk PE30 4LS

All rights reserved.
Printed in Malaysia.

A catalogue record for this book is available from the British Library.

ISBN: 978-1-78637-994-8

Written by:
Harriet Brundle

Edited by:
Emilie Dufresne

Designed by:
Jasmine Pointer

IMAGE CREDITS

All images are courtesy of Shutterstock.com, unless otherwise specified. With thanks to Getty Images, Thinkstock Photo and iStockphoto. Front Cover – VectorShow, Anatolir. 5 – eHrach. 6 – MSSA, Studio_G, Pro Symbols. 7 – Anatolir. 9 – NotionPic. 12 – Elena3567. 13 – matsabe, Elena3567. 14 – 1st Step. 15 – VectorShow, alazur. 16 – miniaria, graphic-line, Oleksandr Derevianko. 17 – miniaria, Antonov Maxim. 18 – Rvector, A Aleksii. 19 – Irina Strelnikova.

CONTENTS

Words that look like **this** can be found in the glossary on page 24.

WHAT IS RENEWABLE ENERGY?

Renewable energy is energy that is made from things that will never run out. These include sunlight, wind and water.

Hi! I'm Bella Bulb and I'm a light bulb.

Renewable energy is often called clean energy because it does not **pollute** our planet. Pollution is bad for our planet, so it's important that we use energy from renewable sources as much as possible.

I need energy so that I can work.

FOSSIL FUELS

Much of the energy we use is **generated** by fossil fuels. Fossil fuels include coal, gas and oil and are found underground.

We all use energy every day.

Fossil fuels are being used faster than they can be **replaced**, and soon they will run out. Burning fossil fuels is one of the largest sources of pollution.

WIND ENERGY

Wind energy is generated by wind **turbines**, which usually have tall towers and three blades. Wind turbines can be small enough to fit on a house or big enough to tower over buildings.

BLADE

TOWER

Hello! I'm Taavi Turbine.

As the wind blows, the blades of the turbine turn around and energy is generated. This energy can then be used for lots of different things.

We're making energy. Look at us spin!

Wind turbines are built in places where it is windy. This might be on land or in the sea. Energy that is created from wind turbines in the sea is known as offshore wind energy.

A group of wind turbines together is called a wind farm. Some wind farms have hundreds of turbines. The more wind turbines, the more renewable energy is generated.

Hi, I'm Taavi. I'm generating the energy you need to shine!

Hi Taavi, I'm Bella. It's nice to meet you.

SOLAR ENERGY

Look at this solar panel, Taavi!

Solar energy is energy we get from the Sun. Solar panels are one way we can **harness** this energy. Solar panels are placed where they will get the most direct sunlight shining on them.

You may have noticed solar panels on the roofs of houses. Although the panels can cost a lot of money, they do not cause any pollution and can save money on energy bills over a few years.

Zzzzz

Solar panels can only harness energy when the Sun is out.

HYDROPOWER

Hydropower is thought to be one of the oldest types of renewable energy. Hydropower uses the movement of water, for example in rivers or streams, to generate energy.

A fast-flowing river, or water falling from a height, such as from a waterfall, can generate lots of energy. The moving water turns the blades of a turbine and the energy is harnessed.

The turbines used in hydropower can sometimes look similar to me!

TIDAL ENERGY

Tidal energy is energy that is generated by the movement of water with the **tide**. As the tide moves in and out, the turbines harness the energy from the movement.

Tidal energy is seen as a more **reliable** source of renewable energy. This is because the tide will always move, unlike wind or sunlight which can be less **predictable**.

Turbines are very useful when it comes to renewable energy!

I'd better move – the tide is coming in!

RENEWABLE
FUEL

Plants are renewable, but oil is not.

Fuels are **materials** that are used to make power. Biofuel is a type of renewable fuel that is often made from plants.

Biofuel can be used to power things such as cars. Biofuel is thought to be much better for our **environment** than fossil fuels.

Biofuel and renewable energy sources are always the best choice.

ROOM FOR IMPROVEMENT

Although renewable energy is better for our planet, it has some problems. If the Sun doesn't shine or the wind doesn't blow, no energy can be generated using solar panels and wind turbines.

I can't work without energy.

In the past, renewable energy has cost a lot of money. More recently, however, the cost has become lower, which means that more people will be able to use energy from renewable sources.

It's important that we keep trying to use more and more renewable energy sources.

HOW CAN I HELP?

Encourage those around you to think about renewable energy options. You can also try to reduce the amount of fossil fuels you use each day.

ON

OFF

All of us can help to save energy by making small changes.

Rather than using the car every day, try to walk or use a bike. Turn off your lights when you're not using them and make sure to turn electrical items off at the socket.

GLOSSARY

INDEX